Our House Was on Fire

To Jennifer –
I hope these poems
make you feel inspired.
—Laura
AWP 2015

Our House Was on Fire

Poems

~~Laura Van Prooyen~~

Laura VanProoyen

 THE ASHLAND POETRY PRESS

Printed in the United States of America

ISBN: 978-0-912592-79-4

Library of Congress Control Number: 2014941525

Author photo: David Frank

Cover photo: Jessica Tampas

Cover design: Nicholas Fedorchak

Acknowledgments

Grateful acknowledgment is given to the editors of the publications in which these poems first appeared:

32 Poems, "Mother of a New Diagnosis"
The American Poetry Review, "Winter Craft"
Blackbird, "Perennial"
Boston Review, "Eighth Stage of Love"
Cimarron Review, "Gone Into the Woods Directly"
The Collagist, "This Child" and "My Incoherent Alphabet"
The Cortland Review, "Repair," "When, Lord, the Sky," and "Bloom"
Crab Creek Review, "Glass"
The Cresset, "Undertow"
Exit 7, "Pine" and "Self-Portrait, Sitting"
The Greensboro Review, "Asking of the Bird What It Cannot Offer," and "October"
James Dickey Review, "After the Weekend Rain"
Meridian, "Migration" and "Understory"
The National Poetry Review, "Revision"
No Tell Motel, "Could Be a Bird," "Happiness," "How Quickly Nothing Is Familiar," "Intersection," and "Undoing Her Hair"
OCHO, "Marsh" and "On the Pier" (as "Wetlands")
Pleiades, "Red Geraniums"
Rhino, "Out of Town"
Slate, "Two Novembers"
The Southern Review, "Decade" and "Our Story in Snow"
Sou'wester, "Continuum" and "Temptation and a School Bus"
Spoon River Poetry Review, "Blue Nude"

"October" appeared on *Verse Daily*.

"Hummingbird" and "Orchard" won a Dorothy Sargent Rosenberg Prize.

This book was written with generous support in the form of grants from the American Association of University Women and the Money for Women/Barbara Deming Memorial Fund, and fellowships from The Ragdale Foundation, Virginia Center for Creative Arts, and Madroño Ranch: A Center for Writing, Art, and the Environment.

I offer special thanks to Philip Levine for nominating this book and to Deborah Fleming for selecting it for the McGovern Prize. Here, I also thank Sheila Black for her generosity, friendship, and particular belief in these poems.

Thank you to the following readers and friends: Marianne Boruch, Joanne Diaz, Jill Alexander Essbaum, Christian Gullette, Ann Hudson, Lynda Jordan, Maurice Manning, Heather McHugh, Rose McLarney, Alison Powell, Deborah Ryel, Allison Seay, Alan Shapiro, Cassie Sparkman, Angela Narcisco Torres, and the entire community of the Warren Wilson MFA Program for Writers.

Thanks to Sarah Wells, for her editorial excellence, and to my colleagues and students at Henry Ford Academy: Alameda School for Art + Design for supporting me both as writer and teacher, and for being open to poetry.

Love to Jack and Pat Van Prooyen. And finally, thank you to my truest friend, Tim Clyne—and our girls.

for Sadie, Jessie & Ivy

Contents

You may ask yourself,"What is that beautiful house?"
You may ask yourself,"Where does that highway go to?"
And you may ask yourself,"Am I right? Am I wrong?"
And you may say to yourself,"My God, what have I done?"

"Once in a Lifetime," Talking Heads

Migration

Listen, then. Quiet as a dream. As the moment
she held her breath to see the man who touched her

all night was not the one next to her sleeping. If
that was a dream. The man she met in the woods

with whom she stood knee-deep in mayapple
naming one hundred birds. On the woodchip path

he took her heart outright and called it a ruby, a painted
rose-breast, a crest, a blood-red crown. Even

without her heart, even within a dream, she knew
to put her plume in his hand was never to go back.

Eighth Stage of Love

Tell me I am not the only one
        who saw the hawk in the tree. Who saw

the bird's swift descent. Once you said
        you wanted to be my adventure. Tell me

now. Here, where shade is scarce. Where
        the sidewalk is burning and dogs

walk with purpose. Remember when you found me
        by the lake and we heard the rain?

How close it came but never reached us? Tell me
        it reached us. It came down

before we had the chance to swim. I don't know how
        to swim and you know that. It came down

and you took my hand. We ran to the house
        we were renting. No, we ran toward the dam.

Remember how fierce the churning? The water
        littered and loud? Last spring

they found that body of a man
        and across his belly the gothic-lettered tattoo:

Cremate Me. That's what I want: a message
        and a journey. Like that, but not exactly.

Do you see? I cannot be the only one who noticed
     that hawk. Or how it perched in the oak

before it ambushed something by our garage. Tell me
     you want to know what's wrong.

This Child

She woke and told me
her dream. She had been
in the kitchen gathering
knives. She
was planning to cut
and eat me. This, she
said, is what bad people do.
Now, how do I begin
to worry about
this? My little tenderloin
snuggles my hip in the easy
chair. I stroke her
hair while she kisses
my arm. We keep
telling the other, *I love you*
and *I love you,* and we do,
though we both know
where the knives are.

Asking of the Bird What It Cannot Offer

The grackles could be a figment. So too, the outdoor café
and the couple under the tree that clatters with noise.

It is morning. With certainty I can say: Here is the sun.

But the man at the table looks like the one I love
who once watched me cut our grass
as grackles swooped in to pick our lawn.

The way he holds his toast is familiar. And look
how he reaches for the woman's hand.

She is turned from him and toward the river, stirring
her coffee, clinking the spoon.

I note this man. And the proximity
                    of the woman to the bridge.

It is then the grackles lift like smoke from a house fire
to fan across the sky.

If this is imagined and the rustling that remains
            is another black bird, I ask it to say it is so.

Happiness

Then there was a sign of happiness: the postman
      blew me a kiss while I raked the leaves.

You've seen this before. Once I wore
      an impossible dress to a party and drank so much

I woke with a mysterious bruise. You should have known
      that was what I called happiness. Not

the bruise, but the not knowing. Anything can happen.
      I like it like that. You show me

the target and insist I put my finger through each hole.
      You are right to think this will impress me.

That it might get the response you're after. But remember
      I am the girl who, long before you,

hopped on the back of some guy's bike never thinking
      he could drive me to the cornfield

and leave me there when he was through.
      It doesn't really matter that I ended up

with only a tailpipe burn. The point is I can't quite say no.
      And neither can you. And who wants to anyway?

Especially when you're not really sure what you might lose.

How Quickly Nothing Is Familiar

First, the headless vireo.
Then the labrador sprung from the brush. And now

the man with his hand between the scruff
and collar leading the dog away.

My daughter runs the worn path. Her pink jacket
bright as bubblegum, or lipstick. Or

the bougainvillea I once potted in Texas
far from these woods

where everything has gone green.
She runs toward the river, a bloom

in a tunnel at the bend where the man
disappears. Before I think to say no.

Mother of a New Diagnosis

How alluring is the pine, its needled limbs bent
heavy with cones. When all was well

I pondered the crown of a distant tree:
bow and sway, sway

and bow, and how an evergreen releases
a soft if imperfect bed

upon a forest floor. I've been quite busy,
old tree, shuffling in lint-covered socks, nesting

in my terry-cloth robe. A sparrow
might be wintering on your bough, but my brooding

is now of lancets and pricks. A series, this,
of blood and measure to tell me

what's next: a quick lick of sugar
for the dangerously deprived? Or must I insist

my daughter lift her hem and choose again
which limb will take the needle?

List

Today I begin with everything
I didn't do yesterday:

Get your hands out of your hair.
Smile more. Stop shaking and pray.

The list for today includes:

Keep your feet dry. Imagine solitude.
Go see the new *Iglesia de Dios*.

But, I step only as far as my porch.
Overhead a V. The geese stall their wingbeats
and glide. A plane breaks the sky
of its silence.

Dios, dios why
does *dios* sound so much better
than God?

Hummingbird

When she crawls into my bed
I feel her quick heart

irregular and fast, too fast
to be my daughter's

whose ribs I feel when I hold her close
to keep her for as many hours

as I can before her heart
defies us both, before

she's a blur at the throat
of the rose of Sharon. Before

only a nodding flower
tells me she was here.

Undoing Her Hair

It was the voice
singing in her daughter's ear
that no one but the child
could hear, then the phantom
in the hall perceived only
by the girl and her cat
that made the mother think
back to the first fever
and spinal tap, to her child
curled up, delirious
at the onset of disease
and know the more
the body fails, the more
the girl speaks of what
the mother cannot see,
so that even as she holds
her daughter on her lap
untangling
blond and twisted braids
she can't believe
she ever thought
this girl belonged to her.

Undertow

For a week I open
the blinds to the tree
and the blue, to the blue behind it.

Should be that this tree is a river,
the pull taking in
whatever will fall,

the bridge that buckles
and disconnects shores, the rocks
dislodged that skid down the bank,

the girls gone out and soon
gone under, the mother who reaches
one, not the other.

Self-Portrait, Sitting

Inside my heart,
I find a set of hands, fingers
intertwined, snaking
down like roots. I find
a tilted roof and a chamber,
hot and still; hornets bang
against the walls, no hole
to buzz through. Inside
my hand shines a mirror
of my heart, reversing
angled rooms, nails holding
windows shut. Even here,
I find a sun-warmed plum.
What darkness beats within
this sweet stone fruit?

Gone into the Woods Directly

If you knew her you might have
stopped her. Said: It's only
an Osage orange. But she seemed

already to know the thorns
when reaching to gather
the brain-shaped fruit. You

might have said: Beware
the red roof, take a big stick,
there are dogs on that road.

She may have answered: I've seen
a black snake, also the bull
and tangle of fern.

And if you knew her, you'd know
she would say this
and still decide to go running.

Understory

Here is what I remember. You pointing
to the fly poised on a bloom. My interest

held by your hand, by your fingers brushing
the wings of the fly and flower. The hair

on your neck coming out of your collar
as you bent to examine the insect, expired.

You motioned to me: *come look, come closer.*
I pulled in near to the curve of your shoulder,

to your pushed-up sleeves and branch-nicked
forearms, to the hush of your breath as you turned

and said: *I've seen this before.* Yes, I thought,
this: the landing, the final moment of flight.

Marsh

This bird is not a symbol
of desire. It is the flicker

and the throat, the unseen
source of song. This bird

is the tremor of a bow,
the vibrato long and drawn.

The symbol of desire
is your hand. Nicked

and knuckle worn. Your
grip could crush this bird's

bones. Which you would do
no sooner than kiss my mouth.

Pine

She opens her heart, a heart
full of needles

and stands at the sink
pulling flesh from bone.

She waits and watches
the broth for boiling

and wonders if
she'll see him again. He,

the stack of wobbly
coins. He, the train

shaking the rails. The pine
bent heavy with cones

whose boughs
reach down to sweep

the roof this morning as
she opens the door

and casts her hope
on the new snow, but

finds the tracks
on her threshold are stars

from raccoons
last night casing the house.

Between What Is Possible
and What Is Desired

This time, in a park
filled with geese and willows
I think I see you
by the bridge. The lagoon

is filled with geese and willows;
your appearance confirms this is not a dream.
There's the bridge, the lagoon,
it's March and snowing.

Your appearance confirms this *is* a dream.
I wear a green scarf, there's a bench,
it's March and snowing and
that is you, I am sure by your gait.

I wear a green scarf, there's a bench
and I resist the urge to answer when you ask:
Is that you? I am sure of your gait,
but I can't say your name.

I resist the urge to answer when you ask
if I think I can see you.
I can't say your name
in the park, this time.

On the Pier

The frog is the gesture of the bird.
Its legs a mirror of flight. A leap
as if a wing. Warbling a pond song.

The pier sets out its planks. The plank
its splintering wear. A sliver flares
in the heel of my palm, the gesture of regret.

No, regret is not quite right. The sliver,
a gesture of desire, or so I thought
of the red-winged bird that really is a frog.

Now, beneath the pier, is that low-pitched
croak called *want*? With the water so thick
with reeds, there is no way to be sure.

After the Weekend Rain

I've been letting this dream
in and out of my day: Us,

at Nine Muses
in Greektown drinking too much.

An afternoon
not so unlike this, except
except.
It is not enough
to say: My hunger is a boat.
It is not enough to say: Your absence

is a flood. Water recedes. Muddied leaves
show where you have been. I drag
a swollen mattress to the curb.

Intersection

Because I cannot call you, you
do not exist. Because

we once ate at Emilio's
I can't drive by

without looking. Today is hot.
I remember you fighting

a woman for the last fan
on the shelf that July. You

may very well be listening
to crickets now. You

may be rocking a child.
I drive my children

past the forest where
we did not go. My skirt

is not so short anymore.
I stop at the red light

where you did not kiss me,
where we did not stop.

Perennial

It can be like this. One day
to wake up thinking *goldenrod. Coneflower.*
Not as suggestions, but directives,
so that I load the children in the car
and go. And it can be

that I hold a trowel
in my hand, thighs scuffed
with dirt and manure, my face
likewise streaked, when I see,
for the first time in years,
someone I once loved.

It is then I wonder
what would have happened
if I rose from bed thinking: *tiger*
or *lily*. Or if
I had stayed
that one night long ago.

But I'm here.
And for a moment, I follow
that staircase again, open the old
apartment door. Stand in the bedroom
on that familiar, uneven floor

with a trowel in my hand, a hole at my feet,
and my daughter, eyes bright like daisies,
asking what I saw.

One Particular Peach

As if this bowl
weren't filled with peaches

or as if
I could resist
the thought of juice that dripped

from my chin into the mouthpiece
while I bit down
to the pit. You moaned and

your breathing got quick.
Then at once the line,

like my heart this morning, grew quiet.

Decade

The life I live is the one you imagined. Yes, in summer,
I pick tomatoes in afternoon heat.
I line my sill with almost-ripe fruit; gauzy

curtains blow against a crooked quartet
of pictures on the wall. Sunlight's been tangling
my hair the same way for a decade,

yet there's no one here you'd know. A girl
gazes into a glass bowl where a goldfish
sucks and spits out stones. Her sister

lounges on the floor, reading aloud
the chapter where wolves circle the heroine's house.
In more than one dream, you've turned to me,

wearing a different face. Once, at the butcher shop,
I stood with arms full of tightly-wrapped packages
when you appeared behind the counter.

You've shown up in the yard, petting my neighbor's dog.
Here, I live my life. The dog is only imagined. Yet,
you go on stroking its fur.

Could Be a Bird

Could be
a bird
would trade

its wings
for hands
for the chance

to grasp
this mango
and lift it
to the tongue

feathers
for fingers
opposable

thumbs
for the chance
to hold

a pencil
and scrawl
goodbye

even
at the expense
of flight.

Solstice

It is not so complicated. I am at the window
grinding walnuts for bread.

The chain link fence
surrounds our dormant stamp of grass.

When you speak, I watch your lips,
or else I can't understand.

This winter is made simple by the cold.
In lean air, the train whistle carries.

Our neighbor's faucet spills out
the Great Lakes, freezes into a rink.

I hear the hockey sticks
smacking ice. I hear blades.

Glass

Because you asked, and the knife
in my hand could not answer, and you refused
my slice of green apple because it was sour,

I could see no other way but to tell you
everything. You pressed
for everything I told you.

Today I pulled out
the frost-blackened tomatoes.
Our daughter poked in the mulch
and found a pair of slugs. For a long time
we crouched and re-routed their trails of slime.

In the afternoon
when I thumbed through the mail, a bird
hit our window, but outside
I couldn't find it on the ground.

I can see how misleading
the glass could be, reflecting trees
and this sky so terrifically blue.

When, Lord, the Sky

When, Lord, the sky
hovers so close
to show its cracks
I try to look

behind the vapors,
but find
I am merely here
among the workings

of this day: The dove
beneath the feeder
pecks, while men
harnessed

to wild contraptions
vacuum
the neighbor's lawn;
what little peace

I've come by, lately,
was in traffic
when I saw a hawk
glide by

a mirrored high-rise,
slicing circles
over the heads
of so many of us

going, for a moment,
nowhere.

Winter Craft

My heart is a pine cone
covered in lard

dunked in a bucket
of mixed seeds, dangling

from the swingset
on a loop of red yarn.

My daughter, mittened
hands on her hips, beams

and calls the birds.

Repair

We're getting a new roof on this old house
where we've been longer
               than we thought we'd be:

our daughter already marking her height to the switch.

The man who once lived here haunts us
             every time the pantry door scrapes
the sloping floor, the clicking hinge
        held by crooked screws.

You curse the splinters in your palm
         from the cheap, warping boards
of the basement stairs
      you're ripping up just now.

But you never look better
       than when you're undoing someone's mistake—

a hammer in your hand,
      the next nail in your mouth.

Continuum

I button your coat this morning but
it was last year the gray and snowing
morning you showed me your finger
swelled and purple that I buttoned
your coat five years ago when the
trees did not reach our house as they
do now leaves in October turning
always school-bus yellow I buttoned
your coat after lovemaking ten years
ago before you drove to New Jersey
for the week you jammed your finger
on a basketball last week it swelled
and this morning maple branches
thrash the awning in the storm after
our lovemaking before you leave and
I button your coat

October

It must be October, when the bones
turn yellow. It must be the yellow

of a mistaken bus. The bee
may have thought: the promise

of nectar. The bee
may have thought: long neck,

a flower. Her hair already
a nest, mistaken. Her hair

already a tangle of bees.
It must be October, a bus

full of children. It must be
the mother digging for bones.

In the Gallery

My daughter sits by the life-sized nudes.
                        I note the contour

of her back. She doesn't know
            I brace for loss, though

I suspect
she knows her body fails.

Last week I saw her draw herself,

            a pack of bees in swarm about
                        a butterfly and its girl.

Waiting Room Window

Black birds line up on the wire.
My daughter can't see them. I can't see

my daughter. She's been wheeled away
stretched out and doped up, smiling.

This is routine. The surgeon's routine,
not mine. The birds have their own

pattern. They rise, dip then drop
onto the wire over the street. The doctor

is fixing my daughter's eyes. I saw a girl
at the pool once. She paddled close to me,

long black hair fanned atop the water,
her eyes turned in so severely,

I felt bad for looking. Still, I looked.

Temptation and a School Bus

Because the neighbor's house is yellow, because I've got a thing
for screens, I sit at the window missing appointments
thinking: the maple has one up on me. It's a gold boat
cruising down the river. A canyon of leaves. A rooster of trees.

The children are due any time with their marching. Their
popcorn eyes and Chiclet teeth. Someone else can deliver
them deliver them deliver waves to my head full of grain.

The cat on my lap is white noise. A warm brick
wrapped in flannel. His ears are trumpets. Nose a stone.
A wheelbarrow of poppies and the children are due any time. I think

I'm hearing voices. The birds have become kazoos. The bus
is spilling out children in halos and rollerskates. Faces framed in fur.
They run like a pack of coyotes. I go, a helium balloon.

Lapse

I'm throwing this day
in reverse. The something

I was seeking is flown,
and my restlessness dazzles

no one, especially not
the crow adorning the peak

of the church roof. God
may have been there, but

he doubled-back. Now
it's cold again. The crossing

guard missing her hat
fluffs her hair in the rear-view

mirror before guiding
young shadows. I've set them

in motion, coming and going
backwards. The tulip, too.

It pulls in its petals, sinks
down its stem, because

I want it to break, again,
unbroken ground.

Revision

Understand, this is a story. You are gone
        and I am home. The viburnum is in bloom.

A convertible speeds past with the top down.
        Wait. Back up. The neighbor invites me

for a ride on his bike. I think yes. I say no.
        Our daughters hear me and laugh. In this story,

we have no daughters. You are a stranger
        and I am the girl. This is the beginning.

You refill, again and again, my drink. We walk
        for hours past row houses. We don't know

where we are. This is the part where I should be scared.
        I'm not. This is the part where you tell me

I'm beautiful, and I believe you. Where you press
        my thigh to your hip. I wipe the rain

from your lenses like a mother, then
        you resist me. You didn't count on the rain.

Or the girl who falls, so quickly, for the stranger
        every time. Understand, the plot

doesn't matter. Only the peak. In this story, you
        are gone a long time. I get a kitten.

It grows. I don't know viburnum from a child's
    pale palm. I refill, again and again, my drink.

This is the beginning. I take off your glasses and lift
    my skirt. I don't know you, but tell you: *resist*.

At the Door

Let there be an apartment
with nothing but a pillow, a window
where I see a fire escape or mountain or anything,
really, where I must answer

no phone or question
just make myself sick with happiness
or loneliness because who can tell the difference.

Let there be a chenille throw, Chinese menus
taped to the wall, a fridge full of beer and my running shoes
at the door. And girls, no

girls rattling the screen, shouting my daughters' names, to find
me in a towel drawing the blinds, stepping on scissors
someone left on the floor.

Blanket

I spot the shredded, knotted
nest of threads, balled-up
again on the floor. The blanket,
almost always preferred
to me, stays unwashed
to keep her smell.
I pick it up and gather
stray tatters, bury them
in the trash. I know it's wrong,
but tucking my daughter in bed
I ask: *If our house was on fire*
which would you choose?
She says: *My blanket, Mom,*
'cause you can run.

Late August

Kids are already out in the street, playing ball.
I fear for the windshield of Debbie's car.
The cantaloupe, this morning, is perfect.
There are not many more breakfasts to be had
on the porch stairs, the air already chill. I didn't see
the new family move in across the street. The boys
use our maple to mark their right-field foul. You said
there's a girl, too. That's a goldfinch in the evergreen
by the empty church. I must be getting old. The shirtless boy
swings his aluminum bat; I'm wearing my winter socks.
A man comes out of the three-flat and zips his car
backwards the length of our one-way street.
I wonder if he's the one who, last night after the music
finally stopped, we heard vomiting in the parkway
when you were holding me because we were cold
and too tired to shut the window or put on clothes.
You were holding me when we were sleeping,
which you never do, and I woke to that surprising sound.

Tango

You loosen my hair, and my head buzzes
like a wall of TVs. I don't know

what I'm thinking. I want
a thrill. I want a tangerine.

Our old cat is forever mewing,
and upstairs a trumpet and flute duet.

Did you happen to see your daughter's
latest drawing? My head is a cracked egg.

But now, you dip me in the kitchen.
Your thigh pressed to my thigh

makes me think of chicken,
and how boys laugh

when they say, *breast*. You hold me
and you kiss mine, so that

however much by day I forget your body,
I find my way back.

Blue Nude

Your husband is painting the room
marine blue and says he wants

to take the roller to you, cover you
bright as an ocean. But you're stuck

on the seashells clinking in his pocket
and the beach spilling out of his cuffs.

The floor piles with sand, or is that
sugar? The white mountain grows.

You should want to put a cherry on top.
You should want to slice it up

like the wedding cake you served
but never did taste. Really, you'd like

to be the sea! To lose your own
rumpled needs. Rush the shoreline

like a wave and recede with a hush,
yes, with his brush against skin.

Plum

Before dawn and I wake to the roller's hushed turning
on the wall. Already you must be flecked
with the bright plum of our bathroom
where we sometimes go, the children young enough
to believe we're cleaning. It's dim,
but from this bed I can make out the tracery
of winter branches at the window, a reminder
of the shadow-theater of which our girls
are so fond. We've seen the falcon
ravage a bare hand, and from nowhere the wolf
lunge to join. A sheet and flashlight,
in the right context, will terrify. In the dark
the sound of your painting mimics breath,
and I listen: grateful we are together even like this.

Variation of Happiness

You should know even as I sipped whiskey
        at the hotel bar, you were sorely missed.

See how it is? Now we tell each other
        everything. Some days we're dying

for something to give. Nothing does
        and sparrows go on yipping at dawn

in forsythia hedges no matter how we thin them.
        Though you're not the only one

to understand flattery will get you everywhere,
        you are the one who caught me

when I tripped on the stairs last night.
        Did you realize your old, tender gesture

split me apart? Your hand around my waist,
        from behind, steadies my clumsy self.

My Incoherent Alphabet

I sit before the page and begin a prayer.
The incoherent alphabet I spin is prayer.

Batter my heart three person'ed God reels
through my head, therein my prayer.

I test my daughter's blood at night. Dark
drops rush through her skin, like prayer.

My mother urges me to read the Bible
to my girls. I read Grimm, say a prayer.

This warning from my love: *Don't drink.*
Keep your pants on. I mix my gin with prayer.

My girl just now comprehends her disease
has no cure; I'm closer to chagrin than prayer.

Here I am, asking for help again. Lord,
your patience must be wearing thin as prayer.

Red Geraniums

Carrying a bucket and three brushes, my mother
leads us through the cemetery. Early spring,
and hostas are just poking up
around the graves. My girls take turns
pumping water, then my mother shows them
which headstones to scrub.
I don't remember coming here much as a child.
Only as an angry teen in the snow, searching
rows of stones for my people,
and upon finding them, smoking
slowly a cigarette. I leaned on this oak,
looking up at the few remaining leaves, listening,
as if to ghosts. My daughter
appears placid, rinsing the name
of my grandfather, whom I never met.
My mother tells stories about him
roller skating and being the first to take
pig insulin in clinical trials.
She's right—we've come a long way
in treating disease. Still, what good would it do
to be spared from sorrow? Resting
on the grassy plot that is to be hers,
my mother tells us to one day plant here
red geraniums, just as a train blows past
on the nearby tracks. On the same rails
that run by her old high school, where I went too,
and where I remember, now,
spring of my senior year, my history teacher
was shot by a student right before lunch.
I thought he was joking

when he staggered backward into class
and fell, then a spot of blood bloomed
from the shirt pocket on his chest.
Later I learned he had turned
in such a way that, somehow, his heart
had been missed. And he lived,
and then lived better than ever before.

On the Discovery Channel

Not long after
my daughter understands

her illness is forever,
we watch caribou migrating

over the arctic plain.
I try to hold her close,

but she turns and cries
about the *stupid, stupid mothers*

as cows swim across the river,
the current washing

the weakest calves away.

Sullenness Is My Daughter's New Posture

Used to be, the air still stinging
with dregs of winter, I'd take my daughter

to the alley and snip branches
from a willow grown wild. We'd gather

sticks of shining, furry buds, stroke them
with chapped fingers, refusing gloves

to hasten spring. If you had asked me,
I would have said we were just passing time—

our small ritual, a way to fill an afternoon hour.
Back in the house, she'd unwrap my hands

from my mug, cover her cheeks with my palms.
What heat I once had to dispel cold.

Two Novembers

In the dark I hear it, the first sign: the cat can no longer jump
into the pedestal sink. His companion already fertilizes
the variegated dogwood in the yard.

This is how my daughter thinks about death, a small ceremony
followed by the hope of swift replacement.

Families living along the high-tension wires report,
more often these days, animals missing. Just last week
a coyote took apart the neighbor's dachshund.

When my father begins to form words after his last round
of seizures, he repeats for two minutes straight: *tasteless tasteless
tasteless.* My first thought is of mashed potatoes and wrinkled
peas I had seen spooned to his mouth. His wife stops the tape
of his muttering with her gentle touch and question: *What, love,
is so tasteless?* He looks slowly from the floor to our faces
and manages to find the word, *everything.*

On my way to the discount store, I go through the forest preserve.
Near the creek I quick-stop the car to point out a coyote
to my daughter. Despite the cold, we roll down the windows
and stay until it lopes out of sight.

Last Thanksgiving, when her grandfather still had words but had
lost inhibitions, my daughter helped him *give the turkey a good one*
stuffing their fists through the hole.

And this is how my daughter thinks about death. They will shave
a patch off the cat. She'll cradle our pet in a towel on her lap and watch
its face when the needle goes in, because she wants to see how it looks.

Orchard

This is not our first time in the orchard. Not
the first time our daughters run from us
among the trees. We are not here so much for apples as to be

where we've been before. Where,
with your father, we once gathered bushels of fruit
and you pulled the girls in the wagon while he rested
                                        on a crate between rows.

The night your father died,
you drew a bath and invited me into the water.

Your response was flesh,
and when your shoulder pressed against my mouth,
I remember thinking you
                        would be easy to bite and bruise.

Belonging

I hardly recognize your stomach, my legs
in this clear water. Something about
the flame and candle, the steam

and flesh. You are right; it feels good
to make the bath so hot
we can barely stand it. And I like

when you tell me what's on your mind,
like how you were disturbed that I asked:
Somos muertos? And you answered:

Si. You want me to assure you,
in our own language, that it was just a dream.

Out of Town

In an elm, a crow stabs the morning
I spend in a quiet hour

without you. If you were here,
the room would smell of pears,

and this indifferent day
would not be reluctant to pass.

Bare trees in this unfamiliar city
remind me that our love

is equal parts desire
and restraint. My hunger

to hear you sharpens my taste.
I want you on the table, knocking

the bowl of green apples to the floor.
In this unfamiliar city, bird cries

are ghostly, like people of the past
who belong neither to you

nor me, but to whole regions lost
to forgetting. Yesterday

when you called, I wanted to say
beauty is wind-worn. To say

in this city, a train sounds
like every other train.

The Streets of My Town Disappear

I go out into the vanishing world
for a walk. Woods soften

with snow, and what's left of the trees
looks like towers, like ruins

of a burned out city eroded by light.
Tired of praising what's lost,

I name things and people I love,
each word rising

from my mouth as a puff
of steam. It's so quiet. Nothing here

resembles my life. My steps,
already, are half-erased.

Our Story in Snow

I thought leaving you in bed
might show you I love you. I'll shovel
the snow this time. You sleep or sit
by the window looking at this fresh expanse
of white. Besides, I've just been thinking
of icicles, how those hanging from our gutters
for the last month have slowly grown long
and luminous. Their harsh beauty
seeming, now, like a metaphor for the years
I did you wrong. I'm sorry there was a time
I contemplated our bookshelf and wondered
who would keep it when we split. This snow
is heavy. My breathing reminds me
of labor—4 a.m. and us pacing
the perimeter of that cold, small room.
You counted and held my hand.
When my body pushed and I shattered
like a mess of stars, or a windshield, or—
I never could describe it—you stayed
beside me, eyes shining with fear. I would say
I'm different now, but probably
I'm not. Except I'm here in my mis-matched
long johns with unbrushed teeth. I'm out here,
clearing this blast of snow from our stairs.

The Sweeping Inside

My daughter walked with me
to the grocery
to keep me from spinning away
in sadness. Even at ten,
she understands a whisk broom
across the nerves.
Introducing her school band,
she fears to speak. At night,
she shakes with the ghost
of her *abuelo* in her head.
When I sat in troublesome silence,
she thought to do a flip
on the swing would bring
some cheer. When it didn't,
we made our way to the store,
where I scan rows of cans,
squeezing her hand that holds me here.

Song of My Morning Walk

This is the day
the screen door has made,
let me rejoice
and walk through it.
The cat with a mouse
lodged firmly in mouth,
runs down the alley
away from me. The morning
is mottled, sky as gray
as the coyote bitch
by the Little League field.
Overhead, a spider web
ties together two oaks.
I float along my quiet street
and hum like high-tension
wires, while under the ground
cicada nymphs graze
on roots. This is the day,
yes, this is the day
of energy coiled in the dark.

Self in the Dark

If I'm honest,
I'm most myself

alone
and in silence.

Clock and sunrise
quiet
your protests!

My heart, too,
resists,
screeching

like a note, blown
by a novice
on her new clarinet.

Solitude,
my black instrument,

how long can I stay
unschooled?

Arch

My daughter perfects
her backbend, curves
into a fluid arc.
Her shirt slides up,
shows each rib
and the hollow spaces
between them.
Her belly sinks,
stretches over her organs,
the one that has failed
and another I know
is leaking, even as
she holds her bridge.

Bloom

It's true, I thought it was funny to ride my bike
in front of the house where the man
would open the curtains, naked.

But, today might be the day
I stop missing my childhood.

This morning, the tiger lilies opened
their throats, the clematis
grown tall as a fifth-grade girl.

I braid my daughter's hair
and remind her not to take the shortcut
through the Laundromat or the alley.

I know the world can be broken,
yet beautiful. I want to believe loneliness

is not menacing, but can be a window
from which I watch her walk away.

Notes

The song "Once in a Lifetime" appeared on the Talking Heads album *Remain in Light* (1980) and was written by David Byrne, Brian Eno, Chris Frantz, Jerry Harrison, and Tina Weymouth.

The first sentence of "October" is adapted from a line in Ana Castillo's poem "My Father Was a Toltec."

McGovern Prize Winners

Laura Van Prooyen, for *Our House Was on Fire* (nominated by Philip Levine)

Catherine Staples, for *The Rattling Window* (nominated by Eamon Grennan)

Robert Grunst, for *Blue Orange* (nominated by Marilyn Chin)

Christine Gelineau, for *Appetite for the Divine* (Editor's Choice, selected by Deborah Fleming)

Elizabeth Biller Chapman, for *Light Thickens* (nominated by Enid Shomer)

Michael Miller, for *The Joyful Dark* (Editor's Choice, selected by Stephen Haven)

Maria Terrone, for *A Secret Room in Fall* (nominated by Gerry LaFemina)

Nathalie Anderson, for *Crawlers* (nominated by Eamon Grennan)

A.V. Christie, for *The Housing* (nominated by Eamon Grennan)

Jerry Harp, for *Gatherings* (nominated by John Kinsella)